THE BEST JOB EVER

Animator

WITHDRAWN

Ian F. Mahaney

PowerKiDS
press.

New York

Published in 2015 by The Rosen Publishing Group, Inc.
29 East 21st Street, New York, NY 10010

First Edition

Editor: Caitie McAneney
Book Design: Katelyn Heinle

Photo Credits: Cover © iStockphoto.com/pafe; p. 5 andresr/E+/Getty Images; p. 6 © iStockphoto.com/GrigoriosMoraitis; p. 7 (top) Bloomberg via Getty Images/ Bloomberg/Getty Images; p. 7 (bottom) http://commons.wikimedia.org/wiki/ File:Pixaranimationstudios.jpg; p. 9 (top) Valerie Macon/Getty Images Entertainment/ Getty Images; p. 9 (bottom) Igor Bulgarin/Shutterstock.com; p. 11 Goodluz/ Shutterstock.com; p. 13 (top) Karramba Production/Shutterstock.com; p. 13 (bottom) Ruslan Grumble/Shutterstock.com; p. 14 Featureflash/Shutterstock.com; p. 15 Alfred Eisenstaedt/The LIFE Picture Collection/Getty Images; p. 17 Alberto E. Rodriguez/WireImage/Getty Images; p. 19 (top) Jordan Strauss/WireImage/ Getty Images; p. 19 (bottom) racorn/Shutterstock.com; p. 20 Ciaran Griffin/Photodisc/ Getty Images; p. 21 Geothea/Shutterstock.com; p. 22 Dikiiy/Shutterstock.com.

Library of Congress Cataloging-in-Publication Data

Mahaney, Ian F., author.
 Animator / Ian F. Mahaney.
   pages cm. — (The best job ever)
 Includes bibliographical references and index.
 ISBN 978-1-4994-0115-8 (pbk.)
 ISBN 978-1-4994-0089-2 (6 pack)
 ISBN 978-1-4777-5923-3 (library binding)
 1. Computer animation—Vocational guidance—Juvenile literature. 2. Animation (Cinematography)—Vocational guidance—Juvenile literature. I. Title.
 TR897.7.M3443 2015
 741.5'8023—dc23
                                      2014031813

Manufactured in the United States of America

CPSIA Compliance Information: Batch #CW15PK: For Further Information contact Rosen Publishing, New York, New York at 1-800-237-9932

Contents

WHAT DO ANIMATORS DO?

Have you seen the movies *Frozen*, *How to Train Your Dragon*, or *Cars*? These are **animated films**, and they're made by people called animators. Animators are very skilled in drawing and using computer programs to make a **series** of images, or pictures, that create motion. If you like to draw or use computers, a job as an animator might be a good fit for you.

Animators start a movie by drawing pictures. Then, they put these drawings together to make it seem like characters are moving and background scenes are changing. Animators understand how people and animals move, so they can trick viewers' eyes into seeing motion.

When we watch animation, we really see many pictures one after the other very quickly rather than moving characters.

WORKING AS A TEAM

Animators are creative people who love bringing pictures to life. Many animators like art and drawing. Many also like working on **projects** with other people.

Animators usually work on animation projects in teams. These projects could be long movies, such as the ones you watch in movie theaters. They could also be television shows or short movies, also called shorts. Some animators work on video games, write computer programs, or create moving images on websites.

Each animator on a team has a different duty. Some animators work for big animation companies such as Pixar. It's an accomplishment to create a finished movie or television show and then watch it.

Based in California, Pixar is one of the biggest American computer animation **studios**. Famous Pixar movies include *Toy Story*, *The Incredibles*, and *Up*.

THE RIGHT EDUCATION

Most animators go to college to study **design**, computer science, or art. Animation studios want to hire animators who've studied and understand these subjects. They also want to hire people who have **experience** working on animation projects, both in and out of the college classroom. Animators need to have computer skills, especially the ability to use programs that make movies and video games.

Some colleges offer programs that focus on animation. Students learn how to draw using computer programs. Then, they learn how to make lifelike movement using their images. You can start your animation education now by taking art classes.

Some animation companies, including Pixar, like to hire animators who study acting. Acting teaches animators how a character moves and what their face looks like when they feel a certain way.

ANIMATOR BIO: JENNIFER YUH

Jennifer Yuh is a Korean-American animator who studied illustration in college. She found a job with DreamWorks Animation and directed the animated hit *Kung Fu Panda 2*.

PORTFOLIOS AND DEMO REELS

Animation students usually complete enough projects in school to create a portfolio. A portfolio is a collection of artwork that a person shows to a company to gain employment. Animation companies like to see an **aspiring** animator's portfolio to get a sense of their skills and style.

An animator's demo reel is even more important. A demo reel is a sample animation that aspiring animators create to show their ability to create movement. A good demo reel shows animation companies that an animator understands how to create motion and capture a character's actions and feelings. Portfolios and demo reels prove an aspiring animator has experience and talent.

One way to gain animation experience is through an internship. Internships are short-term jobs with little or no pay that help a beginner gain experience.

2D, 3D, AND CGI

When an artist draws a picture, the drawing has two **dimensions**. This is called 2D, and it means you can see and measure the length and width of the drawing. When an artist sculpts with clay, it's 3D. In 3D artwork, there are three dimensions—length, width, and depth.

Animators can animate both 2D and 3D images. Computer-generated imagery, or CGI, means using computers to animate images. CGI can be used on both 2D and 3D films, using different programs. To make a 3D CGI film, an animator creates a model of an object or character, which they can then move using the computer.

Some 3D movies require special glasses for viewing. These movies trick your brain into seeing images pop off the screen.

J. Stuart Blackton made the first animated movie, called *Humorous Phases of Funny Faces*, in 1906. Blackton drew faces on a blackboard and filmed them. He stopped the camera to change the face or erase it and draw another face. Stopping a camera to move something or change an image before filming again is called stop-frame animation.

The first feature-length computer animated film was *Toy Story* by Pixar Studios, which came out in 1995.

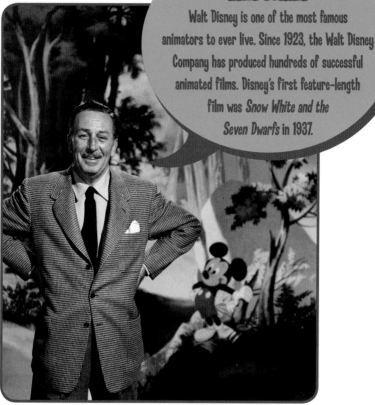

Walt Disney made the first animated film with sound in 1928. It was called *Steamboat Willie* and starred Mickey Mouse. *Steamboat Willie* was less than eight minutes long. Today, animated movies are much longer and more advanced. Many animated movies are feature length, which means full length.

JOBS IN THE MOVIES

Animators who make movies hold many different jobs. Some animators create scenery, or backgrounds, while others create objects or characters. Some animators create storyboards, or plans that show the main actions of the characters. Animators fill in the action between the storyboard's frames so it looks like the characters are moving. An animated film's director watches over all the steps in the production of the animation.

Animators need special skills to animate on a computer, especially when using 3D CGI. Before CGI, animators had to draw each image. That's thousands of images per movie! Using CGI, animators can copy images and make minor changes.

Jennifer Lee became Disney Animation's first female director when she directed the movie *Frozen*. She accepted the Academy Award for Best Animated Feature Film in 2014.

Jennifer Lee

Animators create more than just movies. Some work in television, **advertising**, and the medical field. Some create video games. In all these jobs, animators draw images and combine their drawings to **imitate** motion.

Animators who make television shows work very much like film animators. The projects are often shorter, but many involve several **episodes**. Video game animators use computers to make characters that can be moved by a player.

Medical companies hire animators to make moving images of the human body. Animators use computers to show how bodies work. Animation can be used to show a heart pumping blood or a person moving their arms.

Video game animators need to create a whole world inside their game. The character needs to be able to turn all the way around and move from one location to another, all within a lifelike world.

ANIMATOR BIO: PENDLETON WARD

Pendleton Ward is an American animator who works for Cartoon Network. He graduated from the animation program at California Institute of the Arts. He created the TV series *Adventure Time*, which has won many awards.

JOBS RELATED TO ANIMATION

Many people work together to produce a movie, video game, or television show. Authors write the story and put together a **script** for actors. Voice actors speak the parts of the characters. Music supervisors add music to a film. They either find a perfect song or have one recorded especially for that project. Film directors oversee the whole film, as the stories, animation, music, and voices come together into a final product.

Both animators and illustrators draw pictures to show a story.
Illustrators work on drawings for books and magazines.

Other jobs are related to animation, including computer programming. Computer programmers create websites and programs for different companies. Animators often love art, and other jobs in art include comic strip writers and illustrators.

YOUR DREAM JOB

If you love drawing and computers, a job in animation might be perfect for you. Animators get to work on a team and create something new every day. The movies animators work on sometimes become huge hits. The video games other animators create are sometimes played by millions of people.

It's hard to get a job in animation because there aren't as many jobs as there are animators. Being an animator takes creativity, skill, practice, and the right education. Are you interested in a job as an animator? If you are, you can start taking art lessons and learning beginner's animation now!

Glossary

advertising: The business of trying to sell a product.

animated film: A movie in which individual frames are shown quickly one after another to seemingly create motion.

aspiring: Strongly wanting to achieve a goal.

design: The art of planning the way something will look.

dimension: A measure of length, height, or depth.

episode: One show of a TV series.

experience: Knowledge or skill gained by doing or seeing something.

illustration: The art of creating pictures that help explain a story, poem, or book.

imitate: To appear like.

project: A task.

script: The written story of a play, movie, or television program.

series: A group of similar things that come one after another.

studio: The place where a movie company runs its business.

Index

Websites

Due to the changing nature of Internet links, PowerKids Press has developed an online list of websites related to the subject of this book. This site is updated regularly. Please use this link to access the list: www.powerkidslinks.com/bje/anim